MAGNUS

MAGNUS' SAGA

THE LIFE OF ST MAGNUS
EARL OF ORKNEY
1075 - 1116

Translated and with an Introduction by
HERMANN PÁLSSON
and
PAUL EDWARDS

With wood-engravings by
KATHLEEN LINDSLEY

KIRK SESSION OF
ST MAGNUS' CATHEDRAL
KIRKWALL

ISBN 0 9528164 0 7

First published by the Perpetua Press, Oxford in 1987
Reprinted 1990
This edition published by the Kirk Session of
St Magnus' Cathedral, Kirkwall in 1996

Printed in Great Britain
and distributed from St Magnus' Cathedral,
Kirkwall, Orkney KW15

CONTENTS

LIST OF ENGRAVINGS

FOREWORD

St Magnus of Orkney is not just an interesting historical figure, but an inspiring example whose influence has very contemporary resonances.

The lives of the saints are, of course, much embellished by the hagiographers and the myth makers. Even so, Magnus stands out against the background of his time as a quite remarkable figure. At a time when heroes had names like Thorfinn the Skullsplitter and Eirik Bloodaxe, gentleness was not the virtue that would be immediately associated with public leadership. While we must not present Magnus in the contemporary garb of conscientious objector or Greenpeace crusader, the lineaments of an extraordinary personality are there for all to see.

Magnus could not have secured his position as earl if he had simply been a mild and inoffensive pacifist, but the picture of him reading psalms at sea while battle raged has a winsome integrity about it, especially in the light of his subsequent death. The story of his calm willingness to lay down his life for the peace of Orkney has many echoes of the Passion narrative. The relics of Magnus, which were found in the Cathedral earlier this century and which have been put back into the pillar from which they came, show the axe-mark on the front of his skull that one would expect from the reading of the narrative of his death.

Every generation, of course, reads into the lives of legendary heroes what they wish to find. One is reminded of the words of the Roman Catholic New Testament scholar, George Tyrell, as he commented on Harnack's portrait of the historical Jesus of Nazareth, "The Christ that Harnack sees, looking back through nineteen centuries of

Catholic darkness, is only the reflection of a liberal Protestant face, seen at the bottom of a deep well." At the risk of falling into a similar reductionism, one must say that the love for God, peaceableness, and willingness to make the ultimate sacrifice – while still praying that the cup of martyrdom might pass from him – which Magnus exhibits are truly awesome in their Gospel marks: all the more so because these are the qualities that we desperately need today. If human beings are to live together on this fragile earth, worship, reverence, love and the willingness to sacrifice for others must be seen as necessities rather than idealistic impossibilities. The Skullsplitter of history has been rampant this past century: the finding of new ways is not a luxury.

So Magnus can still be our teacher. This beautiful book can give us inspiration. It was first produced by Vivian Ridler and Hugo Brunner of the Perpetua Press. The Kirk Session of St Magnus' Cathedral is very grateful to them for assigning the publication rights, and to Hermann Pálsson and Paul Edwards for assigning their copyright, to the Session. May all who read this book, and may all who visit the Cathedral which bears his name, be touched by the spirit of St Magnus.

Rev. Ronald Ferguson,
Former Minister, St Magnus' Cathedral
Kirkwall, Orkney

INTRODUCTION

Early Icelandic literature has provided memorable portraits of six northern saints living in the 11th and 12th centuries: they range between the warrior-saint with distinct viking affinities and the scholar-saint, wielder of words not weapons. The first and fiercest of these saints was King Olaf of Norway (d. 1030), known in Orkney as St Ola. He came to the throne when the country was still half-heathen, and he himself had spent his youth as a viking:

> Olaf Haraldsson was twelve when for the first time he went aboard a warship ... Towards autumn he sailed east to Sweden and attacked and laid fire to the whole district, having it in mind that he had good reason to hate the Swedes who had killed his father, Harald. (*Saga of King Olaf the Saint*, Ch. 4)

Not being a man for half-measures, Olaf destroyed all opposition and established Christianity in the realm on the grounds that men are better dead than pagan. As he lived, so he died by the sword, fighting an army of farmers who opposed his tyranny, and killed by his own subjects.

Like King Olaf the Saint, St Knut, King of Denmark (d. 1086), was a military leader confronting disaffected farmers who were eventually to kill him. However, his death took place not on the battlefield, but in a church where he had been attending Mass. The saga records him as singing psalms while his loyal supporters fought to defend him, making no effort himself to kill his assailants and virtually embracing death at the hands of a man he trusted right up to his last moments.

When Eyvind came before the king he bowed. 'Hail, sire,' he said.

The king looked at him but made no reply. Then Eyvind let the tunic fall from his shoulders. Underneath it he had a drawn sword with which he made a lunge at the king, driving it right through his body. The king sank back against the wall asking God to protect him, and died instantly. (*Knytlinga Saga*, or *The History of the Kings of Denmark*, Ch. 58)

It is in keeping with the realistic tradition of the sagas that these two national saints are sometimes shown to be far from saintly, and this, indeed, might be expected of two kings involved in the struggle for political and military power. But even as we move by way of two other sainted rulers of worldly authority, Earl Rognvald (d. 1158) and Earl Magnus of Orkney (d. 1117), towards our two scholar-saints, Bishop Jon Ogmundarson of Holar (d. 1121) and Bishop Thorlak Thorhallsson of Skalholt (d. 1193), realistic elements continue to show themselves in spite of the hagiographic impulse to spirit them away.

Earl Rognvald of Orkney was a very remarkable man, warrior, poet, administrator, crusader to the Holy Land, nephew of St Magnus and founder, in 1137, of his cathedral in Kirkwall. Born in Norway, Rognvald had to fight his way to power and during his twenty-two year reign in Orkney he was involved in many a battle; however, he was to die, not on the battlefield, but on a hunting trip to Caithness, killed by an old enemy at the door of a farmhouse. His obituary gives us this description of him:

> Earl Rognvald was deeply mourned, for he had been much loved in the isles and in many other places too. He had been a good friend to a great many people, lavish with money, moderate, loyal to his friends, a many-sided man and a fine poet. (*Orkneyinga Saga*, Ch. 104)

Such gentle qualities as friendship, generosity, loyalty, popularity, sensibility and moderation mark him out from the type of the warrior-saint, whom he only partly resembles. In one of his own verses he lists his accomplishments, not only the active sports, skiing, rowing and marksmanship, but the more intellectual, chess, along with reading, writing, the ability to interpret runes and, above all, music and poetry. Other poems demonstrate other aspects of this many-faceted man, some of them poems of war, some of seafaring, some of love affairs:

> Once the wine serving wench understood me,
> The touches of my tongue: I was content.
> I loved that good lady, but lime-bound stones
> Crumble: now I cram the hawk with carrion.
> (*Orkneyinga Saga*, Ch. 87)

Thus in the descriptions of these three saintly men of action, one soon detects a tension between the kind of men they were (or perhaps, the saga-narrator wished them to be), and the kind of impression a saint might be expected to convey.

Like Earl Rognvald, the two Icelandic saints, bishops not secular rulers, were interested in music. St Jon had a fine singing voice, played the harp himself and employed a Frenchman to teach music and versemaking at his school. He was famed for his generosity and open-handedness to the poor, and loved by all his parishioners whom he, in turn, loved as if they were his own brothers and sons, we are told. From women, it appears, he kept his distance, even from his wives, for though he married twice he had no children, 'so that we have heard it said, and many believe this, that he remained unsullied by fleshly contact'. (*Jon's Saga*, Ch. 17) St Jon fought no battles and died in his bed: as he lay there after receiving the last sacrament, one of his clerics, an exceptionally good scribe, came to him with a book he had just completed and enquired what price he should ask for it. With his last words, St Jon demonstrated his power to see into the future. 'This is a fine copy,' he said, 'but the man you wrote it for is not the one who will get it.'

St Thorlak, too, lived the life of a scholar and priest:

> It was his custom even as a young man to spend much of his time studying books, though he also often wrote, and in between times, prayed. But when he was otherwise unoccupied he learned from his mother what she could teach him of genealogy and the history of individual people's lives. (*Thorlak's Saga*, Ch. 3)

Like St Magnus, and unlike St Rognvald, Thorlak does not appear to have been a ladies' man. His saga tells how his kinsmen advised him to propose marriage to a certain wealthy widow, a fine young lady; but the night before he intended to ask for her hand, he had a dream. A noble looking man came to him with this warning: 'I know that you intend to take a wife, but there is another bride destined for you, so you must not marry this one.' Thorlak took the advice given him in the dream, and we are told that the subject of dreams was one of his favourites. He is said to have been temperate in his habits, to have eaten little and never taken strong drink in such quantities that he showed the effect of it. We also learn that he was 'so fortunate in the matter of brewing that the ale never went bad once he had blessed it'. He is said to have never spoken an idle word, but he was no killjoy, for he enjoyed storytelling, poetry, music and intelligent conversation. He was Bishop of Skalholt in Iceland from 1176 to 1193, was educated abroad as well as at home, having spent several years in Paris and Lincoln at his studies, and like St Jon, he died quietly in his bed.

We now come to Earl Magnus, the subject of our saga, uncle to Earl Rognvald and distant cousin of St Jon. Magnus' father, Earl Erlend Thorfinsson, had fought against King Harold of England at the Battle of Stamford Bridge, in which King Harald Sigurdarson of Norway was killed, in 1066, shortly before King Harold of England himself died at the Battle of Hastings. The life of St Magnus shows him as sharing some of the features of the warrior-saints, but also to have close affinities with the scholarly St Thorlak and St Jon. A description of him is to be found in Chapter 7 of this translation, but we should like to quote here from the rather fuller account of him in *Orkneyinga Saga*:

St Magnus, Earl of Orkney, was a man of extraordinary distinction, tall, with a fine, intelligent look about him. He was a man of strict virtue, successful in war, wise, eloquent, generous and magnanimous, open-handed with money and sound with advice, and altogether the most popular of men. He was gentle and agreeable when talking to men of wisdom and goodwill, but severe and uncompromising towards thieves and vikings, putting to death most of the men who plundered the farms and other parts of the earldom. He had murderers and robbers arrested, and punished the rich no less than the poor for their robberies, raids and other transgressions. His judgments were never biased, for he believed divine justice to be more important than social distinctions. While he was the most generous of men to chieftains and others in powerful positions, he always gave the greatest comfort to the poor. He lived according to God's commandments, mortifying the flesh throughout an exemplary life in many ways which, though revealed to God, remained hidden from the sight of men.

His intentions were clear when he asked for the hand of a girl from the noblest family in Scotland, celebrating their wedding and afterwards living with her for ten years without allowing either to suffer by way of their lusts, and so remaining chaste, without stain of lechery. Whenever the urge of temptation came upon him, he would plunge into cold water and pray to God for aid. (*Orkneyinga Saga*, Ch. 45)

The reader may well feel at this point that the hagiographical purpose of the saga-narrator has taken over, and might compare it with the open acknowledgement of erotic life in the poems of St Rognvald. Similarly, there is the episode in the life of King Knut the Saint, in which Knut takes a fancy to the wife of a priest with whom he is staying, and gets as far as her bed, but is so mortified by the extempore sermon

14

she delivers that he feels ashamed at his own lack of restraint:

> '... It is an effort all the same to act against one's desires, but this is very little compared with the great sufferings Our Lord Jesus Christ bore for our sake,' [said Knut]. With that the king went away and got another bed for the night. (*Knytlinga Saga*, Ch. 31)

As a result of episodes such as this, though St Knut may appear, from a strictly spiritual or hagiographic viewpoint, to suffer from unsaintly imperfections, he is humanised by his awareness of them and his vulnerability to them, to the considerable advantage of the saga as secular narrative.

But to return to St Magnus: according to a late 12th century summary of the history of the Kings of Norway, he was eighteen years old when King Magnus Barelegs took him along on his expedition to the western isles, described in Chapter 3 of our translation. He demonstrates at this early age his saintly virtues by refusing to fight 'for he had no quarrel with anyone there. "God will shield me," he said.' To emphasise his point, 'Magnus took out his psalter and chanted psalms throughout the battle, and though he refused to take cover, he wasn't wounded.'

However, Magnus is not always painted so white. In the longer account of the Life of St Magnus which we discuss below, we are told this:

> It appeared for some years that he might well turn into a bad lot and take up the viking life with thieves and fighting men, living by plunder and violence and involved with other men in killings: but one could truly believe that he had been more encouraged by others' wickedness than actually wicked himself. (*Magnus' Saga II*, Ch. 8)

15

That there is more to the life of St Magnus than the picture of a meek and saintly figure is also suggested by the passage in this saga—Chapter 7 below—which tells of his killing of a chief named Dufniall, and the burning to death of a man called Thorbjorn in his house. But as a ruler of Orkney in troubled times, he could hardly have survived, let alone fulfilled his task as a just legislator, without the kind of severity ascribed to him in the account of his character given in *Orkneyinga Saga*. Though his inclinations may have been towards the spirit of the scholar-saints, his secular responsibilities were bound to align him, in some degree, with the warrior-saints such as Olaf and Knut.

There are three distinct but closely related texts telling the story of the life of St Magnus, and we discuss them in more detail in our note on the texts and sources (p. 45): but all three go back to a Latin *Vita*, now lost, along with a book of St Magnus's miracles. Almost invariably, the miracles are performed on behalf of people from Orkney and Shetland, and are about the cure of the blind, the insane, lepers, and cripples or people suffering from broken bones. Also, these miracles are performed in a low key, on behalf of working people with nothing of the spectacular about them. These miracles are placed, understandably, at the end of the narrative, and contribute to the steady change of tone, from its opening description of family conflicts within the circle of power-seeking kings and nobles—much in the spirit of *Heimskringla*, *Knytlinga Saga* and *Orkneyinga Saga*—to a preoccupation with divine matters in the spirit of hagiography. As we have suggested, the transition is not altogether easy since the heroic or viking elements remain traceable in the life of the saint, and the effort to dispense with or conceal them may lead to a spiritual elevation of the hero which, to some readers, may appear more of a dehumanisation. *Orkneyinga Saga*'s placing of St Magnus in the context of a wide range of leaders, along with the militant warrior-saint, Earl Rognvald, and a gallery of princes and farmers, gives that saga a scale which this short life of St Magnus is bound to lack. The drama of the life and death of St Magnus, and his miraculous interventions, may arouse less intense feelings in those who anticipate the fierce conflicts and worldly issues which have come to typify our expectations of saga-narrative. But we must set some of these expectations aside and acknowledge the very different spirit of the northern scholar-saint, closer to Thorlak and Jon than King Olaf or King Knut. For not only is St Magnus from the start a man of peace, he is also identified with the world of scholarly learning and habits of contemplation. In the longer version of *Magnus' Saga* we are told,

> He settled down early at school to the study of holy scriptures and other learned matters that men thought it most important to cultivate knowledge of. Magnus was quiet and attentive, pliable and good-natured towards his father and mother, and to his teachers. (*Magnus' Saga II*, Ch. 4)

Consequently, the moments of drama in this saga are not of violent action, but of spiritual intensity and vision. It is appropriate that the place of his death, far from taking on a grim or ominous atmosphere, 'turned into a fair meadow, and he himself won the beauty and greenness of Paradise, which is called the Land of the Living'. It is appropriate too that, instead of the revenge that one might expect in the great saga tradition, Magnus' mother forgives his killer, Earl Hakon, in a striking but understated scene. Earl Hakon has just killed St Magnus but since he had been invited to a feast by Magnus' mother, Thora, he turns up and begins to drink heavily, Thora herself serving him. All she asks is that she might be allowed to bury her son:

> The earl fell silent. He began to think things over and to feel the burden of his terrible crime. He looked at her and wept.
> 'Bury your son,' he said, 'wherever you wish.'
>
> (p. 33)

The reader is left unsure whether Hakon's tears are a result of drink or self-recrimination, but perhaps there is something of both allowed for, since, though there is no mention of it in this short saga, in the longer account in *Orkneyinga Saga*, Earl Hakon, having made a pilgrimage to the Holy Land and bathed in the river Jordan, 'grew to be a fine administrator and brought firm peace to the land'. (*Orkneyinga Saga*, Ch. 52)

Perhaps the most striking example, however, of the way this narrative can dramatize its material in the best traditions of the great sagas, is the scene in which St Magnus is given a portent of his imminent death, while on his way to meet Earl Hakon and establish the peace between them he so earnestly desires. In spite of a calm sea and shallow water, a gigantic breaker crashes down upon the stern of the ship, where Magnus is seated. He recognises it as an omen, but, against all the pleas of his men, insists on completing his journey: 'I shall go, sure enough,' the earl replied, 'our journey will end as God wills.' (pp. 28–29)

The incident suggests the world of supernatural portents so characteristic of the saga tradition, creating a powerful image of the undercurrents of violence at work, of which the saint is aware, but from which he refuses to back away, putting his faith in his God, and his own spirit and sense of destiny. In this, he is not so far removed from his heroic, pagan ancestors as his saintliness might lead us to expect. The cult of St Magnus spread widely, as indicated not only by the three accounts of his life but also by the devotional works in Latin and in Gaelic which we have included in this book as appendixes (pp. 46 and 50) and by the number of churches which honour him. In addition to St Magnus' Cathedral, Kirkwall, three Orkney churches, in Birsay and on Egilsay and Stronsay, are dedicated to St Magnus; five are dedicated in Shetland, two in Caithness, one in the Faroes, seven in Iceland and three in England.

Those who want to know more about the life and times of the saint than *Magnus' Saga* provides should in the first place turn to *Orkneyinga Saga: The History of the Earls of Orkney*. It is now available, in our translation, in the Penguin Classics but it was originally published by The Hogarth Press in 1977 whose permission to quote from it we acknowledge. We also recommend John Mooney's book *St Magnus, Earl of Orkney* (Kirkwall, 1935) though it is out of print. Readers of Icelandic should turn to Magnús Már Lárusson, 'Sct. Magnus Orcadensis Comes', in *Saga: Tímarit Sögufélags* (Rit 24) III. Bindi, Reykjavík 1960–63, pp. 470–503. Much more readily available is George Mackay Brown's novel *Magnus* (The Hogarth Press, 1973), the culmination of this author's imaginative exploration of the subject, and which in turn inspired Peter Maxwell Davies' chamber opera *The Martyrdom of St Magnus*.

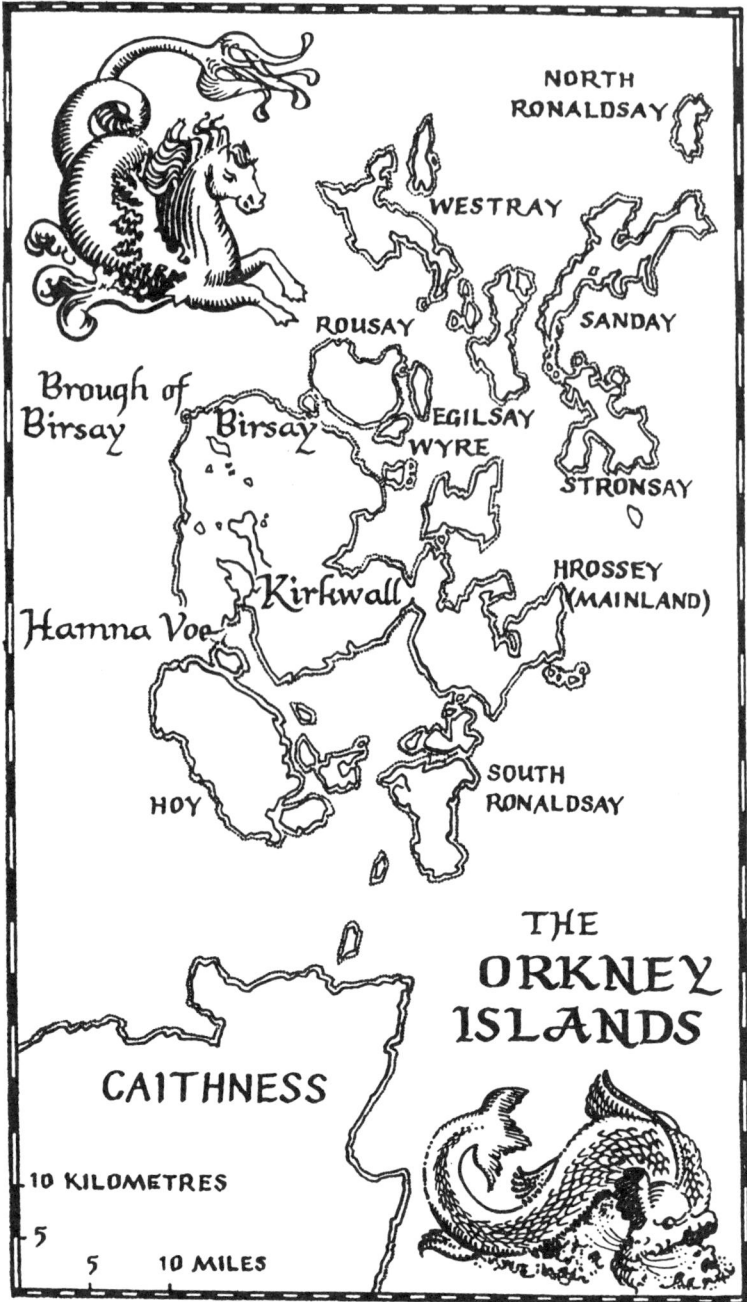

NORTH
RONALDSAY

WESTRAY

SANDAY

ROUSAY

Brough of
Birsay   Birsay   EGILSAY
                                WYRE

STRONSAY

Kirkwall

HROSSEY
(MAINLAND)

Hamna Voe

HOY   SOUTH
             RONALDSAY

THE
ORKNEY
ISLANDS

CAITHNESS

10 KILOMETRES

5

5   10 MILES

MAGNUS' SAGA

1. FAMILY BACKGROUND

Ruling over Orkney was an earl called Thorfinn, son of Sigurd Hlodvirson. He was married to Ingibjorg, nicknamed 'the Earls' Mother', who was the daughter of Earl Finn Arnason and Bergljot, daughter of Halfdan, son of Sigurd Sow and Asta.

Earl Thorfinn's sons by Ingibjorg, Paul and Erlend, took over power in Orkney on the death of their father. Both were tall, handsome men, taking much after their mother's side of the family, as well as being shrewd and modest.

Earl Paul married a daughter of Earl Hakon Ivarsson and of Ragnhild, daughter of King Magnus the Good. Their son was Earl Hakon.

Earl Erlend married a woman called Thora, daughter of Sumarlidi, son of Ospak whose mother was Thordis, the daughter of Hall of Sida. The sons of Erlend and Thora were Erling and Magnus, and their daughters were Cecily and Gunnhild, who was the mother of Earl Rognvald Kali.

2. A FAMILY DIVIDED

The brothers Paul and Erlend ruled in Orkney with concord and goodwill, but their sons Hakon and Erling grew up to be very arrogant, though Magnus took things more easily. They were all of them strong and talented, but Hakon wanted to lord it over his kinsmen, for he thought himself more high-born on his mother's side. But his cousins thought differently, and as a result they could not be in each other's company without the risk of a quarrel. The earls did their best to bring the family together and a meeting was arranged, but once talks had begun it became clear that each of the earls favoured his own son, so no agreement could be reached. At that, friends intervened and they settled matters between them by dividing the Isles, half to each of the brothers as the arrangement had been in the past, and that was how matters stood for a while.

But as time went by after the settlement, Hakon grew to be such a bully and bore down so hard on those serving under Earl Erlend, that they fell out once again, confronting each other with large numbers of men. Havard Gunnason and other friends of the earls tried to make peace between them, but Earl Erlend refused to come to terms as long as Hakon was around, and their friends thought their quarrel had become a matter of grave concern: so the farmers pleaded with Hakon to leave the islands rather than stand in the way of peace, arguing that the wisest counsel would be for him to go east overseas and visit his numerous distinguished kinsmen in Norway and Sweden. Under such persuasion, because of the envy he bore against his kinsmen in the Isles, and his wish to learn something of the life-style of other chieftains, Hakon set out from the Isles and sailed eastward.

3. A MAN OF PEACE

When King Magnus Barelegs brought his army west over the sea, as told in his saga, he came to Orkney, took captive the Earls Paul and Erlend, and sent them east to Norway, making his own son Sigurd overlord of the islands with regents to govern the earldom. King Magnus declared that the earls would never rule in Orkney as long as he was King of Norway.

From Orkney, King Magnus sailed on to the Hebrides taking with him Earl Erlend's sons Erling and Magnus, and Hakon the son of Earl Paul. As King Magnus was approaching Wales, he encountered a large fleet in the Menai Strait under the command of two brother-earls called Hugh the Stout and Hugh the Proud, sons of King Kostnama of Ireland. No sooner had they met than the king sailed into battle, but while his men were readying their weapons, Magnus Erlendsson sat himself down. When the king asked why he was sitting around and not seeing to his weapons, Magnus replied that he had no quarrel with anyone there.

'So I'm not going to fight,' he said.

'Then take up your weapons for your own protection,' said the king.

'God will shield me,' answered Magnus. 'I shall not be killed if he wishes me to live, but I'd rather die than fight an unjust battle.'

'Get below deck then,' said the king, 'don't lie around under people's feet, if you haven't the courage to fight. I don't think it's your faith that puts you off fighting.'

Magnus took out his psalter and chanted psalms throughout the battle, and though he refused to take cover, he wasn't wounded. It was a long hard battle, but in the end Hugh the Proud was killed and the Welsh took flight, having suffered heavy losses: and though King Magnus lost many a brave man there, and others died later of their wounds, he won the day.

4. MAGNUS ESCAPES

King Magnus had appointed Magnus Erlendsson his cup-bearer, and he used to serve at the king's table, but after this battle the king took a strong dislike to him and said that he had acted like a coward. One night when King Magnus's fleet was lying at anchor off Scotland, Magnus Erlendsson decided it was his best chance to get away and jumped overboard. He swam ashore and ran into a wood, wearing nothing but his underclothes, stumbling about and scratching his feet for he had no shoes on. He had arranged his berth so that it looked as though someone was sleeping there. When he could walk no further he climbed up into the branches of a large tree, bound up his foot, and hid there for a while in the branches.

Next morning, as the king's men were sitting at breakfast, the king asked where was Magnus Erlendsson, and was told that he was still asleep in his berth. The king told them to wake him, saying they would find it was not only sleep that kept him lying in bed longer than usual. When they came to his berth, however, and found him missing, the king told people to make a search and gave an order to let slip the bloodhounds. The dogs were set loose, took the scent at once, raced into the wood and stopped under the tree where Magnus was hiding up in the branches. One of the dogs circled round the tree barking. Magnus had a log in his hand and threw it at the dog, catching it on the flank, at which the bloodhound put its tail between its legs and ran back to the ship with all the other dogs following behind. The king's men could see no sign of Magnus.

He hid in the forest for some time, but in due course he emerged and went to join the court of King Malcolm of the

Scots where he stayed for a while, though he spent some of the time with a certain bishop in Wales, and now and again with various friends in England. But as long as King Magnus was alive, he did not go back to Orkney.

5. THE EARL'S DEATHS

When King Magnus came back to Orkney after his raids, he heard news from Norway that Earl Erlend had died at Trondheim and been buried there, while Earl Paul had died and been buried at Bergen.

In the spring, King Magnus gave Earl Erlend's daughter Gunnhild in marriage to Kol, son of Kali Saebjarnarson, in compensation for the death of his father, Kali having died of wounds received in the Menai Straits. Her dowry consisted of some property in Orkney including a farm at Paplay.

According to some people, Erling the son of Earl Erlend was killed in the Menai Strait, but Snorri Sturluson says that he met his death in Ireland, alongside King Magnus in Ulster.

When the news of King Magnus's death reached his son Sigurd in Orkney where his father had left him to govern the earldom, he thought his prospects of peace overseas in the west were not very good, so that same autumn he sailed east to Norway with those troops which, having followed his father to Ireland, had made their way back home. On his arrival in Norway he was made king there together with his brothers, Eystein and Olaf.

6. EARL HAKON AND EARL MAGNUS

A year or two after King Magnus was killed, Hakon son of Earl Paul sailed to Norway from Orkney. He went to see the brothers and they gave him a good welcome for he had been a dear friend to their father King Magnus. The brothers, the sons of King Magnus, gave Hakon the title of earl as well as all the authority in Orkney that belonged to his birthright. Then he sailed back west, took charge of the whole of Orkney, and ruled alone there for some time.

Shortly after Hakon had come to power in Orkney, Magnus Erlendsson returned from Scotland to claim his inheritance. The farmers were delighted, for Magnus was well-liked and he also had many friends and kinsfolk there who were very keen for him to seize power. His mother was married to a man of excellent family called Sigurd, and their son was called Hakon Karl. They had a farm at Paplay.

When Earl Hakon heard that Magnus had arrived, he gathered his forces and refused to share the earldom, but friends intervened and it was arranged that subject to the approval of the King of Norway, Hakon would give up half of the earldom. Then Magnus set off east to Norway and met King Eystein and King Olaf, King Sigurd being away on pilgrimage to the Holy Land. The kings gave Magnus a good welcome and handed over his patrimony to him, half of Orkney and the title of earl. After that, he sailed back west to his earldom where all the people received him well. He and Hakon settled matters between them, and there was true peace and prosperity as long as their friendship lasted.

7. EARL MAGNUS

As a leader, Magnus was outstanding, courteous in manner and strict in morals, wise, victorious, eloquent and majestic. Everyone sang his praises. He was open-handed with money and sound with advice, brave in battle and loyal to his friends. He punished theft, plundering and other crimes with severity, and robbers and vikings he had put to death. Often he gave lavish gifts to great men, but to the poor he always offered deep consolation for the sake of God. God's commandments he observed strictly in every way, chastising himself at all times. It is said that he lived with a woman for ten years, yet they both remained chaste, for whenever temptation came upon him he would plunge into cold water and pray to God for support.

Earl Magnus and his kinsman Earl Hakon had joint charge of the defences of Orkney for some time, during which they got on well together. Poems composed in their honour tell how they fought against a chieftain called Dufniall, said to be the son of Earl Dungad, the Earls' second cousin, and killed him. There was a man of some importance called Thorbjorn whom they killed at Burra Firth in Shetland. People say they attacked him in his house and burnt him to death inside.

8. DISCORD

Earl Magnus and Earl Hakon had not ruled long in Orkney before it so happened, as it often will, that malicious people began to stir up bad feeling between them, and it was to Earl Hakon that the more ill-starred men were drawn, who did all they could to destroy their friendship. But in the past, Hakon had been deeply envious of the popularity and the noble authority of Earl Magnus.

Two men in particular staying with Earl Hakon, called Sigurd and Sighvat Sock, did most of all to cause trouble between the earls, and the campaign of slander ended up with the cousins gathering forces and attacking one another. They travelled to Mainland where the people of Orkney had their place of assembly, and as soon as they landed they formed up ready for battle. Most of the noblemen of the Isles were with them, and there were also friends on both sides who intervened charitably to reconcile them.

The meeting took place in Lent, shortly before Palm Sunday, and since there were men of goodwill involved it so happened that the earls agreed to these terms, that such men of goodwill should arbitrate between them and that the peace meeting would take place on Egilsay after Holy Week. Each of them was to bring two ships to the meeting and an equal number of men, and each swore to keep whatever agreement might be reached at the meeting.

9. A PORTENT

After Easter they made preparations for this journey. It is said that Earl Magnus summoned all the best men in his earldom, particularly those he thought most likely to help improve matters between himself and Earl Hakon, and once he was ready he set off for Egilsay. As they rowed away on a calm sea, a breaker rose high over the ship steered by the earl and crashed down upon it into the stern where he was sitting. His men were taken aback, for no one had ever seen such a breaker before, and there was deep water beneath them.

'It's not surprising that you should be shaken by such a strange incident,' said the earl. 'My intuition tells me that it forebodes my death. Perhaps what was once prophesied will now come to pass, that the son of Paul will commit a ghastly crime. We must reckon with the possibility that my cousin Hakon isn't going to be entirely honest with us.'

The earl's men were distressed by what he had said and

urged him to watch out for his own safety and not risk meeting with Earl Hakon.

'I shall go, sure enough,' the earl replied. 'Our journey will end as God wills.'

10. A TRAITOR

Now we must tell of Earl Hakon: he gathered a large force of men with eight fully equipped warships just as if he were going into battle. Once his troops were assembled, he made it clear that he meant to settle the matter between Earl Magnus and himself, so that only one of them would live to tell the tale. Plenty of his men liked this idea, and had a good many harsh things to say, the most unpleasant of these coming from Sigurd and Sighvat Sock. Then they started to pull hard on the oars.

Havard Gunnason, a friend of both earls and related to them both by marriage, was aboard Hakon's ship. Hakon had told him nothing of the scheme, but once Havard realised what the earl was determined to do, he jumped overboard and swam to a small uninhabited island, having no wish to become involved.

11. PREPARATIONS

When Earl Magnus saw Earl Hakon sailing up with eight ships, he knew that he must expect treachery and went ashore with all his men up to the church, where he passed the night. His men offered to defend him.

'I'm not risking your lives to save my own,' said the earl, 'and if there's to be no peace between me and my kinsmen, then things must go according to the will of God.'

To his men, it looked as though everything was turning out just as Magnus had predicted when the breaker came crashing down on them: but since he had foreknowledge of his own life-span, either because of his wisdom or by divine revelation, he had no wish to avoid a confrontation with his enemies. For the sake of his faith, he went to church and prayed devoutly, committing himself into God's hands.

In the morning he left the church with two companions, and went down to a secluded spot by the sea, where he prayed to God. Some people say that before Earl Magnus had set out from the church, he had a mass sung for himself and took holy communion.

12. OFFERS

In the morning, Earl Hakon and his men hurried ashore straight up to the church looking for Magnus, but not finding him there they began to scour the island for him. When Earl Magnus saw them, he called out, telling them where he was. Once Earl Hakon caught sight of Magnus, he and his men rushed towards him.

'You've not done well, kinsman, to break your oaths,' said Magnus, 'though you've acted more from other men's wickedness than from your own. Now,' he said, 'I suggest you choose one of three courses. First, that I should travel to Rome, or even as far as Jerusalem, to visit the holy places. I'd take two ships with me to carry all we'd need and do penance for both our souls, and I'd swear, moreover, never to return to Orkney while I live.'

But Hakon would not agree to this, so Magnus spoke again.

'Now that my life is in your hands,' he said, 'I know that I've often transgressed against God, for which I must make repentance: also, I realise how unseemly it would be for you to kill me. So send me to our friends and have me placed under guard with two men to keep me company, and you can be sure that I'll never escape from confinement unless you wish it.'

Earl Hakon and his men were quick to turn this down, and found plenty of reasons why it was unacceptable, so Earl Magnus spoke yet again.

'There's still one thing more,' he said, 'and God knows, I'm more concerned with your good name than with my good health: have me mutilated or blinded, and so cast me into a dungeon.'

'Those terms I'll accept,' said Earl Hakon, 'and make no more conditions.'

At that the chieftains jumped to their feet.

'We're going to kill one or the other of you,' they said. 'We're not putting up with both of you as rulers any longer.'

'Since you're taking such a firm line in the matter,' said Earl Hakon, 'I'd much prefer to stay alive and rule.'

That's how their conversation was reported by a reliable man called Holdbodi, one of Earl Magnus's two companions there. He said, too, that Earl Magnus showed great steadfastness of mind when the words just quoted were used by his adversaries, for he spoke neither in resentment nor in anger. Then he knelt down to pray, covering his face with his hands and shedding many tears in the sight of God.

13. MARTYRDOM

Once Earl Magnus had been sentenced to death, Earl Hakon told Ofeig his standard-bearer to behead him, but he refused angrily. Then Hakon ordered Lifolf his cook to do it, but Lifolf began to weep out loud.

'You mustn't weep,' said Magnus, 'it's not manly. A deed

31

like this can only bring fame. Keep a steadfast mind, you can have my clothes and weapons according to the laws and customs of our ancestors. Don't be afraid, you're doing it against your will, and the man who gives the order sins more gravely than you.'

Then Earl Magnus took off his tunic, gave it to Lifolf, and asked leave to pray. This was granted, whereupon he prostrated himself on the ground, committing his soul to God and offering himself as a sacrifice. He prayed not only for himself and his friends, but for his enemies and killers, forgiving them with all his heart for their crimes against him. He confessed his own sins before God, praying that his own soul might be washed clean by the spilling of his own blood, then placed it in God's hands, praying that He would send His angels to meet him and bear him to the Heavenly Paradise. As he was being led to his execution, he spoke to Lifolf.

'Stand right in front of me,' he said, 'and strike me a hard blow on the head. It's unfitting for a chieftain to be beheaded like a thief. Take heart, poor fellow, and don't be afraid. I've prayed God to grant you his mercy.'

With that he crossed himself and stooped to receive the blow, and took a single stroke on the middle of his head, and so his soul passed away to Heaven. The place where Earl Magnus was beheaded was rocky and overgrown with moss, but soon God revealed how worthy he was in His eyes, for the spot turned into a fair meadow and he himself won the beauty and greenness of Paradise, which is called the Land of the Living. Afterwards a church was built there.

Earl Hakon would not permit Earl Magnus's body to be brought to church.

14. BURIAL

Well-informed people say that after the peace-meeting on Mainland, Earl Magnus's mother, Thora, had invited both earls to a feast on their return from the meeting on Egilsay. On the appointed day, after the killing of Earl Magnus, Earl Hakon went to the feast, and Thora herself served him at table. When the drink was beginning to take effect on the earl, Thora came up to him.

'I was expecting both of you,' she said, 'and now only one has come. Now you must do something in the eyes of God and men that will please me: be a son to me, and I shall be a mother to you. I'm sorely in need of your mercy, so let me have my son borne to the church. Hear my prayers now, just as you yourself would hope to be heard by God on the Day of Judgment.'

The earl fell silent. He began to think things over and to feel the burden of his terrible crime. He looked at her and wept.

'Bury your son,' he said, 'wherever you wish.'

Soon after that, the body of Earl Magnus was carried to Birsay and given burial at Christ Church, which Earl Thorfinn had built.

15. MIRACLES

Not long after the burial, a bright, heavenly light was often seen at night over the grave of Magnus. Then people began to pray to him in time of trouble when they found themselves in peril, and for those who had prayed, all difficulties were soon overcome. People would often be conscious of a heavenly fragrance over his grave, and recovered their health there, so the sick began coming from Shetland and

Orkney to keep vigil at his graveside, and there they were cured of their illnesses. But as long as Earl Hakon was alive, no one dared make all this public. The story goes that the men most deeply involved in the betrayal of Earl Magnus died cruel and violent deaths.

This happened at the time William was Bishop of Orkney, and the episcopal seat was at Christ Church, Birsay, where the Holy Earl Magnus was buried. For a long time the bishop doubted the earl's holiness and hid the news from the people.

16. EARL HAKON'S RULE

After the killing of Earl Magnus, Hakon took over the whole of Orkney and made all those who had previously served Earl Magnus swear oaths of loyalty to himself. He grew to be a powerful ruler, and made those of Earl Magnus's friends who had been most hostile to him in his dealings with Magnus pay heavily for it in taxes. Some years later, Hakon set out on a long journey and travelled south to Rome where he was given absolution for his sins by the Pope. His pilgrimage took him all the way to Jerusalem, where he visited the holy places and bathed in the River Jordan, as is the custom of palmers. After that he returned to his realm.

He grew to be a fine administrator and brought secure peace to the land, making new laws for Orkney which increased his popularity so that, in time, the people of Orkney would accept no one but Hakon and his offspring to rule over them.

There was a farmer to the north in Shetland called Bergfinn Skatason, who was blind. He travelled south to Orkney and kept vigil at the grave of the Holy Earl Magnus; two cripples, called Sigurd and Thorbjorn, kept vigil with him. The Holy Earl Magnus revealed himself to them all and gave them back their health. On another occasion, twenty-four people kept vigil at Earl Magnus's grave, and all were cured of whatever ailed them.

A number of people said to the bishop that he should speak to Paul Hakonarson, ruler of the isles after the death of his father, asking permission to translate the holy relics of Earl Magnus, but the bishop's response was cool. Though the bishop was often reminded in his dreams that he should acknowledge the saintliness of the earl, he refused to believe it; but eventually he was compelled by divine chastisement to pay honour to the miracles and holiness of Earl Magnus.

17. BISHOP WILLIAM

It happened one summer that Bishop William sailed east on some business to Norway, and set off home in the autumn, reaching Shetland around the beginning of winter, but then the weather deteriorated and grew stormy. When for most of the winter the wind remained unfavourable for getting back to the Isles, the bishop despaired of returning to his seat before spring. Should the bishop be in a position to sing mass at home next Sunday, asked the captain, would he admit that Earl Magnus was a saint? The bishop agreed, rather more from necessity than in accordance with his vows. But as soon as agreement had been reached, a favourable breeze blew up and so they set sail for Orkney, reaching home before the following Sunday. Everyone kept praising God and his holy martyr Earl Magnus, but a number of people have testified that still Bishop William would not agree to translate the holy relics of Earl Magnus until it so happened one day, there at home, that the bishop found he could not make his way out of the church because he had suddenly gone blind, nor could he find the door until he repented his lack of faith and wept bitterly, praying to God that he might come to the grave of Earl Magnus. Once there, he prostrated himself flat on the ground and vowed to translate the holy relics of the earl the moment he regained his sight. No sooner had he finished his prayer than his sight was restored there beside the grave.

18. SANCTIFICATION

Afterwards, the bishop gathered together all the wisest and most distinguished men in Orkney, and at a great gathering at Christ Church on Birsay the holy relics of Earl Magnus were translated. The bones had nearly reached the surface. The bishop had them washed, and had one knuckle tested three times in consecrated fire, in which it did not burn but took on the colour of burnt silver. Some people say that the bone took on the shape of a cross. Many miracles were performed there by the holy relics of Earl Magnus.

Then clergy took the holy relics and enshrined them and placed them above the altar: that was on St Lucy's Day, before Christmas, twenty years after the killing of Earl Magnus, and his death is celebrated on the 16th of April. Next, Bishop William decreed that both days should be held sacred throughout his bishopric and from that time forward he held the Holy Earl Magnus in great affection.

William was the first Bishop of Orkney and remained in office for sixty-six years.

19. MORE MIRACLES

There was a respectable farmer on Westray called Gunni who dreamed that the Holy Earl Magnus came up and spoke to him.

'Tell Bishop William that I want to leave Birsay,' he said, 'and go east to Kirkwall. I trust that God in his mercy will grant me this, that the sick may be cured of their ills if they go there with true faith. Speak out boldly when you give an account of this dream.'

When Gunni woke up, he hadn't the courage to speak about the dream because he was afraid that Earl Paul would be angry. The next night, Earl Magnus appeared to him once more in a dream, telling him to describe the dream at a time when the largest number of people would be present.

'And if you don't,' he said, 'you'll be punished for it in this world, but much more in the next.'

Waking, Gunni was filled with terror and set off for Mainland to see the bishop. He described the dream before a large congregation at the episcopal mass, in the presence of Earl Paul. The people all urged the bishop to translate the holy relics to Kirkwall, just as Earl Magnus had asked, but Earl Paul sat there without saying a word and flushed deep red.

Afterwards, Bishop William led an imposing procession east to Kirkwall taking along the holy relics of Earl Magnus, and placed the holy reliquary above the high altar of the church that stood there at the time. In those days, the market town of Kirkwall had only a few houses but since then it has grown considerably. Afterwards, a good many people kept vigil there in the church beside the holy relic and were cured of their sufferings as long as they invoked Earl Magnus in true faith.

A little later, Bergfinn Skatason made a second trip south from Shetland, bringing his son who suffered from leprosy, and they kept vigil by the holy relics. Then Bergfinn donated a large sum of money to the Holy Earl Magnus. On the third night of the vigil, while they slept, it seemed to them both as if the earl stroked Halfdan's body and restored his good health. To Bergfinn it also seemed that the earl touched his eyes.

'You shall recover your sight,' he said, 'exactly as it was at its sharpest, for you came here in true faith, and gave a great deal of money for the glory of God, and never doubted my saintliness.'

And when Bergfinn woke, he could see.

20. YET MORE MIRACLES

There was a man called Thord Dragon-Jaw who was a tenant of Bergfinn the farmer. He was threshing corn in a barley-shed on the eve of St Magnus' Day in winter when just around sunset Bergfinn came out and told him to stop work.

'It's not often that you think I'm working too late,' said Thord.

'Tomorrow,' replied Bergfinn, 'we have to observe mass-day as well as we know how.'

With that, he went away, but Thord carried on working as hard as he could. A little later, the farmer came back and spoke to Thord quite angrily.

'I'm not at all pleased that you're still working,' he said. 'When the holy relics of Earl Magnus were tested and enshrined, today was made a holiday by law. Stop at once.'

But Thord carried on working just as before. When the people of the household were just about to finish their supper, in came Thord. He was dressed in miserable rags, and at once he began drinking. After he'd had a drink he went insane and had to be tied up quickly. He stayed that way for six days, then Bergfinn made a vow on his behalf, offering half a mark of silver to the shrine of Earl Magnus, and a three-night vigil by Thord were he to be cured. The very same night the vow was made, Thord recovered.

There was a man called Ogmund, farmer Bergfinn's nephew. A cross-beam fell on his head and fractured his skull badly. Bergfinn made a vow on his behalf, casting lots to determine whether to promise a pilgrimage to Rome, the freeing of a slave, or a gift of money to the shrine of Earl Magnus. As it turned out, money was to be given to the shrine, and Ogmund was healed, whereupon Bergfinn the farmer gave half a mark of silver to the shrine as promised.

There was a man called Amundi Illugason who suffered badly from leprosy. He went to the Holy Earl Magnus, kept vigil over him, and prayed for a cure. The Holy Earl Magnus appeared to him in a dream, passed his hands over his body, and gave him back his health.

A man called Sigurd went out of his mind and had to be sown up in a hide, but after he was taken to the Holy Earl Magnus he got back his health.

There was a man called Thorbjorn who went quite insane, but when he was taken to Earl Magnus he recovered his health.

There was a man called Sigurd who belonged to Fetlar in the north. His hand was so badly crippled that the fingers were bent over into his palm, but when he went to the Holy Earl Magnus he was completely healed.

There was a woman called Sigrid Sigurd's-daughter who had been blind from infancy. When she was twenty her father took her to the Holy Earl Magnus and had her keep vigil there offering a great deal of money for her recovery, and she regained her sight.

39

Another woman called Sigrid broke her leg in two: she was taken to the Holy Earl Magnus and there she was healed.

A third woman called Sigrid used to stay with Thorlak who farmed at Baliasta. On the eve of Magnus-mass, though the rest of the household observed the feast-day, she carried on sewing. When Thorlak asked her why she was working so late, she said she would leave off. Later, he came back and asked her why she was behaving so badly.

'Get out,' he said, 'you're not working here any longer.'

She said there was only a little more sewing to be done, but carried on working till it was dark. When people were getting ready for supper she went out of her mind and had to be tied up. Thorlak made a vow on her behalf, and lots were cast whether he should offer a pilgrimage to Rome, freedom for a slave, or a donation to the shrine of Earl Magnus. The answer was for a donation. Thorlak took her to Earl Magnus, where she recovered her health, and later she went on a pilgrimage to Rome.

There was a man from Orkney called Thorkel who fell down from the top of his barley-stack, badly injuring one side of his body. He was carried to the Holy Earl Magnus and there he recovered his health.

There was a woman called Groa who went out of her mind. She was taken to Earl Magnus, where, after recovering her health, she spent the rest of her life.

Two men, one from Orkney and the other from Caithness, stole some gold from the shrine of the Holy Earl Magnus. Gilli, the Caithness man, was drowned in the Pentland Firth, and the other went insane, confessing in his madness what they had done. Then a vow was made on his behalf that he would go on a pilgrimage to Rome were he to recover at the shrine of Earl Magnus. Afterwards he was taken there and recovered.

In England once, there were two men staking money heavily on a game of dice and one of them had lost a great deal. So he then staked a cargo boat along with everything else he owned. When the other man threw first and got two sixes, this man we're speaking of thought his chances not very promising, and prayed to the Holy Earl Magnus not to let him lose. Then he made his throw. One of the dice broke, and he got two sixes and an ace, so that he collected all that was at stake, and later gave a great deal of money to Earl Magnus.

After Earl Rognvald Kali, nephew of the Holy Earl Magnus, had come to power in Orkney and settled down, he had the ground-plan drawn up for St Magnus' Cathedral in Kirkwall and hired builders for the work. The structure progressed rapidly and well: it is a remarkable building, on which great pains were bestowed, and later the holy relics of Earl Magnus were transferred to it. Many miracles continued to take place there. Nowadays it is the episcopal seat, the same that used to be at Christ Church, Birsay.

There was a man called Eldjarn Vardason, a farmer up north in Kelduhverfi with a wife and a large number of children. During a famine he became destitute and sick, so he was unable to cope. He grew so weak, he could no longer walk and had to be driven about from farm to farm. In the spring, after Easter, it so happened that he had been driven all day Thursday and Friday through to Saturday without having anything to eat. About three o'clock on the Saturday afternoon he arrived at a priest's house and spent the night there, and next morning when people went to Matins he asked to be carried to the church, which was done for him.

After Matins, people went back to the house in between services, but Eldjarn was left lying out in the church where he had been made comfortable. He felt so weak he thought it must be the end. He started thinking about how things had once been, when he had saved so much money, and he said a prayer that touched him so deeply that he was moved to tears. He made a vow then, to fast for six days if God would give him better health, and promised to observe the fast before St Olaf's Mass and St Magnus' Mass.

After he had made his vow, people came back to the church. The priest sang the Mass, and as the epistle was being read Eldjarn fell asleep. People there thought he was going to die.

In his sleep he had a vision. He thought he saw a bright light in the choir which moved across towards him, and in the light he saw a handsome man who spoke to him.

'Eldjarn,' he asked, 'are you very weak now?'

'That's how it feels, though maybe it isn't so,' he answered, as it seemed to him. 'But who are you?'

'I'm the Holy Earl Magnus Erlendsson,' the man replied. 'Do you want to be well again?'

'Yes, I do,' he said.

'King Olaf the Saint heard your prayer, and the vow you made to us both for the recovery of your health. It was he who sent me here to make you well, as he himself had gone west in the fjords to cure a woman there who had made a vow to him.'

Then Earl Magnus began passing his hands over Eldjarn's body. When Eldjarn woke up the gospel had begun and he asked the men sitting next to him to help him stand.

'What's the point of helping you up if you're so weak?' they asked.

'I think I'm feeling better now,' he answered.

They took hold of him and helped him to his feet, and he stood for the rest of the gospel and right through the Mass, after which he went to the priest and described the miracle, how God had granted him his health. Everyone praised God for the mercy He had shown, to honour the Holy Earl Magnus. May He bestow mercy upon us and the remission of sins in the name of the Lord Jesus Christ, who with the Father and the Holy Spirit will live and reign as God eternal.

AMEN

TEXTS AND SOURCES

There are three distinct but closely related texts telling the story of the life of St Magnus, including his miracles: *Orkneyinga Saga* (mainly chapters 34–57); *Magnus' Saga I* (*Magnuss Saga Skemmri*), the 'shorter version'; and *Magnus' Saga II* (*Magnuss Saga Lengri*). *Orkneyinga Saga* is the oldest of the three, originally composed late in the 12th century and revised c. 1230–40. *Magnus' Saga I*, the present volume, is evidently based on the revised *Orkneyinga Saga*, though it includes certain material not found in the earlier work. It has been suggested that its composition dates from around 1250, and it survives in a late 14th century manuscript. *Magnus' Saga II* was, like *Magnus' Saga I*, written in the north of Iceland and contains several miracles not found in the two earlier versions. Further texts dealing with aspects of the life of St Magnus are the different versions of *King Magnus Bareleg's Saga*. Finally, there is a poem in Icelandic called *Magnus Diktur* based on *Magnus' Saga II* and dating from the 15th century.

Ultimately, the source of all three versions of the life of St Magnus is a Latin *Vita* composed by a 'Master Robert'. Robert is referred to several times in *Magnus' Saga II* as 'Master Robert who composed and created the saga of the Holy Magnus in Latin', but this *Vita* is irretrievably lost though there are brief Latin summaries extant, one being the *Legenda de Sancto Magno* to be found in *Íslenzk Fornrit XXXIV Bindi, Orkneyinga Saga* ed. Finnbogi Gudmundsson, Reykjavík, 1965; the same volume contains the Icelandic texts of the two versions of *Magnus' Saga*, the shorter one of which we have translated in this volume.

Magnus' Saga II states that Robert wrote his account twenty years after the death of Magnus: the most reliable Icelandic annals date this 1116, though it has been argued by Magnús Már Lárusson (*Saga*, 1962) that there are good reasons to identify the date of the martyrdom of St Magnus as 16 April, 1117, so that the *Vita* of Robert would have been written in 1137. Now at this time, other things were happening not unconnected with the writing of the saint's life. Earl Rognvald, Magnus' nephew and later himself to become a saint, was made Earl of Orkney, and it was he who translated St Magnus' remains to Kirkwall, and began building the cathedral there. It seems almost certain that these events were related to the composing of the *Vita* of Master Robert. Very tentatively, it has been suggested that Robert may have been Robert Cricklade, who wrote a Latin life of Thomas á Becket c. 1173–4. Robert was a Canon in Cirencester c. 1130–41, and a Prior in Oxford 1141–74, and he is known to have visited Scotland. The life of St Magnus in the versions which we have (and so presumably in their Latin source) bears a certain similarity to the life of Becket, Earl Hakon functioning in much the same relationship to Magnus as Henry II to Becket.

APPENDIX I

These hymns are taken from services in Latin used at festivals in St Magnus' Cathedral, Kirkwall. They were published in Gudbrand Vigfusson's Icelandic text of *Orkneyinga Saga* and in *Icelandic Sagas*, Vol. III (Rolls Edition). The English translations were made by Ernest Marwick and published, with the Latin originals, in his *An Anthology of Orkney Verse*, Kirkwall, 1949. They are reprinted here by permission of the executors of Mr Marwick.

HYMN AT LAUDS

Exultemus concrepantes sonora melodia
Sancti Magni venerantes martyris insignia,
Ejus digna praedicantes post palmam miracula.

Odor manat en unguenti, alabastrum frangitur,
Quovis morbo gravescente salus vera redditur
Plebs concurrit, fit egenti cuiquam quod petitur.

Leprum mundat, et furorem pellit ab amentibus,
Contuendi dat vigorem privatis luminibus,
Mutis fandi praebet morem, gressum claudicantibus.

Ferro vincti relaxantur, surdi simul audiunt,
Casu fracti mox sanantur, mala quaeque fugiunt,
Naufragantes liberantur dum procellae saeviunt.

O quam probat hunc beatum ossis ejus ustio,
Bis fit auri crux crematum os, sed ossis tercio
Crux fit os ejus sacratum, tam miro commercio.

Magne pater famulorum tibi supplicantium,
Sordes terge delictorum, fidem firma mentium,
Adeptores praemiorum quo simus coelestium.

Laus perennis Trinitati, salus, virtus, gloria,
Uni decus Deitati, mirâ cujus gratiâ
Sui cuncti majestati serviunt per saecula.

AMEN

Exultantly our ringing voices blend
In praise of Magnus, since whose holy end
Are wonders done which all our thoughts transcend.

The urn is broken, but the fragrance steals
To sick and suffering, whom its odour heals;
Swift comes the answer when the suppliant kneels.

Lepers are cleansed, mad souls made calm and wise,
And sight comes back once more to sightless eyes;
The dumb find speech, the impotent arise.

The slave casts off his chains, the deaf can hear;
All wounds are healed, all evils disappear;
Saved are the shipwrecked from the waters drear.

Thrice was the saint revealed: like blazing gold
His bones endured the fire, then took the mould
Of Christ's own Cross, most glorious to behold.

Great Father of all men who bow to Thee,
Make firm our faith, from sin Thy servants free,
That in Thy heaven our high reward shall be.

To God, the Three in One, Eternal Praise;
To Him be Glory, whose constraining grace
Compels the endless service of our race.

                                        AMEN

47

ANTIPHONS AT MATINS

Magnus ex prosapiâ magnâ procreatus,
Actum vitâ moribus major est probatus.
Praedis vacans primitus pravorum instinctu
Ut Paulus convertitur in viae procinctu.

Saulus ecce Paulus fit, praedo fit patronus,
Persecutor factus est plebis pastor bonus.
Vir sactus in comitem digne sublimatus
Carnem per continuos domat cruciatus.

Justus, pius, humilis, et modestus
Iste suis praefuit exemplis honestus.
Magnus inter caeteros gratiâ divinâ
Plenus fulget velut stella matutina.

Vir Sanctus ad propria reversus componit
Cum Hacone perfido, qui fraudem disponit,
Expetit ecclesiam, quâ fraude compertâ
Ut pararet hostiam se Christo spe certâ.

Hostes turbat Comitis mora salutaris,
Hostiâ dum refici expectat altaris;
Sanctum trahunt, rapiunt, templum irrumpentes,
Sacro plenum pabulo extrahunt amentes.

Haconis presentiae Magnus presentatur,
Sitit agni sanguine lupus fore satur,
Protulit sententiam ut morti tradatur,
Et lictori traditur ut hanc exequatur.

Favus stillans frangitur mellis dans dulcorem
Mala quaeque fugiunt cujus per odorem.
Surdi, muti, precibus Magni reparantur,
Claudis data sanitas, leprosi mundantur.

Ferro vincti martyris ope relaxantur,
Naufragantes nexibus mortis liberantur.
Fit moestis laetitia, aegris medicina,
Spes firma periculis, salus in ruinâ.

Magnus, descended of a noble race,
Yet deemed more great for holy deeds and grace:
Reared among pagans, but in youth made bold
To glory in the Cross, like Paul of old.

As Saul, made Paul, becomes the faithful friend
And shepherd of the flock he once did rend,
So Magnus all his dignity abjures
And fiercest scourging of the flesh endures.

Just, godly, humble, with a modest mien,
Well in his life the perfect life was seen;
Endued with grace divine, he shone afar
Beyond all others, like the morning star.

Soon was the covenant that the Saint had made
With faithless Hakon brutally betrayed;
And Magnus, deeming that his hour was nigh,
Knelt by Christ's altar and prepared to die.

Short shrift was given, while the Earl, intent
On higher things, partook the sacrament:
But one short prayer, then violently his foes
Their bitter malice to his prayers oppose.

Like to a lamb the Holy Magnus stood:
The wolfish Hakon thirsted for his blood:
Sentence is given—a shameful death decreed,
And to a low born churl assigned the deed.

The Saint is gone, but o'er his relics still
Does heavenly incense rise, to ward from ill:
Before his shrine are deaf and dumb restored,
The lame arise, cleansed is the leprous horde.

Still shall the Martyr set the prisoner free
And save the shipwrecked from the raging sea,
Give joy for sorrow, from all pains release,
Make strong in peril, bring to the stricken peace.

APPENDIX II

Manus Mo Ruin is one of the Gaelic poems collected during the latter part of the 19th century by Alexander Carmichael, and published, along with his translation, in *Carmina Gadelica: Hymns and Incantations*, in 1900. It was reissued by Oliver and Boyd, Edinburgh, in 1928.

MHANUIS mo ruin,
Is tu dheanadh dhuinn iul,
A chuirp chubhraidh nan dul,
　　Cuimhnich oirnn.

Cuimhnich a naoimh nam buadh,
A chomraig 's a chomhn an sluagh,
Cobhair oirnne 'n ar truaigh,
　　'S na treig sinn.

Tog ar seilbh mach ri leirg,
Casg coin ghioirr is coin dheirg,
Cum uainn fuath, fath, feirg,
　　Agus foirne.

Cuartaich tan agus buar,
Cuartaich caor agus uan;
Cum uap an fhamh-bhual,
　　'S an luch-fheoir.

Crath an druchd o'n speur air crodh,
Thoir fas air feur, deis, agus snodh,
Dubhrach, lus-feidh, ceis, meacan-dogh,
　　Agus neoinean.

O Mhanuis nan glonn,
Air bharca nan sonn,
Air bharra nan tonn,
Air sala no fonn,
　　Comhn agus gleidh sinn.

<pre>
        *
      * * *
        *
</pre>

O MAGNUS of my love,
Thou it is who would'st us guide,
Thou fragrant body of grace,
 Remember us.

Remember us, thou Saint of power,
Who didst encompass and protect the people,
Succour thou us in our distress,
 Nor forsake us.

Lift our flocks to the hills,
Quell the wolf and the fox,
Ward from us spectre, giant, fury,
 And oppression.

Surround cows and herds,
Surround sheep and lambs;
Keep from them the water-vole,
 And the field-vole.

Sprinkle dew from the sky upon kine,
Give growth to grass, and corn, and sap to plants,
Water-cress, deer's-grass, 'ceis', burdock,
 And daisy.

O Magnus of fame,
On the barque of the heroes,
On the crests of the waves,
On the sea, on the land,
 Aid and preserve us.

HERMANN PÁLSSON studied Icelandic at the University of Iceland and Celtic at University College, Dublin. He was Professor of Icelandic at the University of Edinburgh, where he taught from 1950 to 1988. He is the General Editor of the New Saga Library and the author of several books on the history and literature of medieval Iceland; his more recent publications include *Legendary Fiction in Medieval Iceland* (with Paul Edwards) and *Art and Ethics in Hrafnkel's Saga*. Hermann Pálsson has also translated *Hrafnkel's Saga*, and collaborated with Magnus Magnusson in translating *Laxaela Saga, The Vinland Sagas, King Harald's Saga* and *Njal's Saga* for the Penguin Classics.

PAUL EDWARDS read English at Durham University, Celtic and Icelandic at Cambridge, and then worked in West Africa for nine years. He was Professor of English and African Literature at Edinburgh University until his death in 1992. He wrote several books on Icelandic studies with Hermann Pálsson, and published books and articles on African history and literature, and on English literature.

Hermann Pálsson and Paul Edwards have also translated *Egil's Saga, Orkneyinga Saga, Seven Viking Romances* and *Eyrbyggja Saga* for the Penguin Classics, *Knytlinga Saga (The History of the Kings of Denmark)* for Odense University Press, and *Vikings in Russia* for Edinburgh University Press.

KATHLEEN LINDSLEY was born in Gibraltar and had a widely travelled childhood, followed by Fine Art training in Newcastle-on-Tyne. Drawn to the west coast of Scotland by its wild, mountainous beauty, she established her studio on the Isle of Skye in 1978.

She is a member of the Society of Wood Engravers, and has demonstrated the versatility of the medium with her designs for pub signs, letterheads and commercial illustration. Her other work for private presses includes the illustrations for *St Frideswide: Patron of Oxford* (Perpetua Press 1988).